GET READY TO BLAST OFF!

Rockets get space exploration off the ground. Without the powerful thrusts from rockets, nothing can escape the Earth's gravity. Everything would be stuck here.

When we think about rockets, we normally think of sending astronauts into outer space. Rockets are also used to launch long-range space vehicles that conduct experiments and send valuable information back to earth.

The most common use for rockets is to place satellites in their correct location in space. Information from satellites lets us know what kind of weather is headed our way. In addition, phone calls and even television programs are often bounced off satellites and relayed to the comfort of your living room!

While the rocket in this kit won't get to outer space, it *will* give you an idea of the science involved, and it *could* inspire you to grow up and become a rocketeer!

We strongly suggest you read through this book in order, but if you just can't wait to try your rocket, the instructions and safety information are on pages 8-10.

1

The History of Rocketry

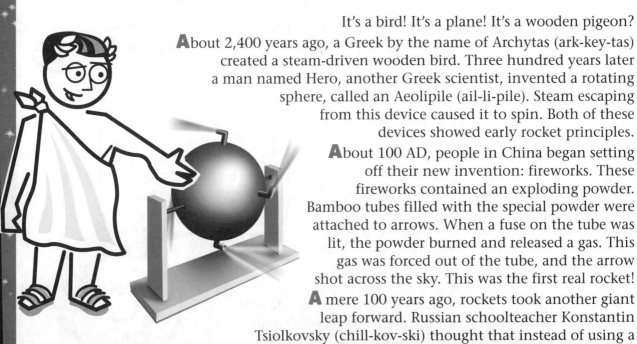

It's a bird! It's a plane! It's a wooden pigeon? About 2,400 years ago, a Greek by the name of Archytas (ark-key-tas) created a steam-driven wooden bird. Three hundred years later a man named Hero, another Greek scientist, invented a rotating sphere, called an Aeolipile (ail-li-pile). Steam escaping from this device caused it to spin. Both of these devices showed early rocket principles.

About 100 AD, people in China began setting off their new invention: fireworks. These fireworks contained an exploding powder. Bamboo tubes filled with the special powder were attached to arrows. When a fuse on the tube was lit, the powder burned and released a gas. This gas was forced out of the tube, and the arrow shot across the sky. This was the first real rocket!

A mere 100 years ago, rockets took another giant leap forward. Russian schoolteacher Konstantin Tsiolkovsky (chill-kov-ski) thought that instead of using a powdered fuel, a liquid fuel like gasoline would allow rockets to travel greater distances. Liquid fuel burns faster than solid fuel, so the gases produced escape faster.

   Building on the work of Tsiolkovsky was an American named Robert Goddard, who is called "the father of modern rocketry." Goddard's rockets used a liquid fuel that burns faster than gasoline, and he changed the basic design of all rockets. Rockets now traveled higher and faster, and could also be controlled. Goddard added a parachute to the rocket so it could safely return to earth. This meant that expensive testing equipment could be added to a rocket, as it wouldn't be destroyed when the rocket landed.

Try This:
Blow up a balloon. Pinch the mouth of the balloon, then release the balloon into the air. How far did it travel? Try this again, using a paper clip to squeeze the end of the balloon so only a little air escapes when you let go. Did the balloon go farther this time?

After All, It Is Rocket Science!

Sir Isaac Newton:

In 1687, an English scientist named Isaac Newton developed three *Laws of Motion*. He believed that there are forces acting on objects that make the objects move. Newton's theories are the foundation of our understanding of the behavior of objects acted upon by forces, and help to explain how and why your rocket works.

Newton's Three Laws of Motion:

FIRST LAW: An object that is moving tends to keep moving in the same direction unless a force comes to change the behavior of that object.

SECOND LAW: An object moves in the direction of the force being applied to it. The amount of force needed to move an object is directly related to the object's mass (amount of material in the object) and acceleration (how fast something increases in speed).

THIRD LAW: For every action, there is an equal and opposite reaction.

How do these laws work together to make rockets fly? Well, the rocket fuel burns, and hot gases shoot out the back of the rocket, making the rocket move forward *(third law)*. Most rockets are fairly heavy, so it takes a large force—the gases shooting out—to make a rocket speed up to the point where it can escape the Earth's gravity *(second law)*. Once the rocket starts moving, it keeps moving in a straight line until another force makes it turn or stop *(first law)*.

Rocket Design

Science plays an enormous part in the design of a rocket. For instance, the fins on a rocket keep it moving smoothly through the air, as well as keep it from tumbling. However, this only works where there is air, not in the emptiness of space. For rockets that actually head into outer space, scientists had to come up with new ways to steer the rocket, using Newton's laws. One way to do this is to use small extra rockets on the outside of the main rocket. When the engines on these rockets are turned on, they push gases out on one side of the rocket and the rocket turns away from that side. Another way to turn a rocket is to have a moveable nozzle. The nozzle turns so that the gas comes out in one direction and the rocket goes in the other direction. That's why there is such a thing as *rocket science!*

How Baking Soda and Vinegar Power Your Rocket

Your rocket has both a solid and a liquid fuel. The solid fuel is baking soda, which scientists call *sodium bicarbonate* (so-di-um bi-car-bon-ate). The liquid fuel is vinegar, a mixture of water and a chemical called acetic (ahs-eh-tik) acid. When these two chemicals combine, you have a chemical reaction. This reaction makes some new chemicals: water, carbon dioxide gas, and a harmless chemical called *sodium acetate* (ahs-ah-tate), which is sometimes added to potato chips to make them taste like vinegar. The chemical that makes your rocket move is carbon dioxide. This odorless, colorless gas escapes through the opening at the back of your rocket and sends the rocket off into the air. Your body also produces carbon dioxide gas when you breathe in and out, and it is the bubbly part of soda pop. No, you can't make soda pop by blowing into juice with a straw! Nice idea, though!

VINEGAR

BAKING SODA

Try This:

Place about 1 cup of vinegar into a 1-liter soda bottle. Use a funnel to put 2 tablespoons of baking soda into a balloon. Carefully stretch the top of the balloon over the mouth of the bottle so that you have a tight seal. Now lift the balloon up so that the baking soda goes into the bottle, and watch what happens. The baking soda mixes with the vinegar, and carbon dioxide gas is released. This gas inflated the balloon! If you pulled the balloon off the bottle, the gas would send the balloon flying through the air, just like it does your rocket.

Alka-Seltzer™

Your rocket can also be fueled with antacid tablets such as Alka-Seltzer™. These contain mainly two chemicals, sodium bicarbonate and citric acid. You must add water, and the chemicals react to make carbon dioxide gas, water, and a harmless chemical called sodium citrate.

Using Your Rocket

Safety First:

Make sure you understand these rules before using your rocket.

1. Only launch your rocket in a wide-open space outdoors, with no small children nearby.
2. After you have added the fuels to your rocket, quickly move away from the launch pad. Never stand directly above the rocket or look straight down at it on the launch pad. It's a good idea to wear protective safety goggles when you set off your rocket.
3. Do not aim your rocket at people, windows, cars, or other objects that can be damaged or broken.
4. Rinse your rocket with water after each firing. Carefully wash the plastic parts of your rocket with warm, soapy water when you are finished experimenting.
5. Do not add any other fuels except the ones described in the instructions.
6. Do not eat, taste, or drink any of the rocket fuels.

Do you know a song about rockets? I bet you do! In "The Star Spangled Banner", you sing about "the rockets red glare". If it weren't for Francis Scott Key, who wrote the words that became the United States of America's national anthem, we might not have known that the British fired rockets against the Americans in the War of 1812!

Let's Build It!

Now that you know why your rocket works, let's build one. Remove all the pieces from the bag.

1. This is your base. The hollow section in the middle of the base is where you add your liquid fuel (vinegar).

2.

The hollow, yellow tube with the red foam nose cone is the body of your rocket. The hollow section is where you will add your solid fuel (baking soda).

3.

Your rocket also has three fins. Attach these to the rocket body by sliding them up the yellow tube and clicking them into place.

Blast Off!

Okay, now let's have some fun! Your rocket is designed to work with two kinds of fuel. See which of the fuels below give your rocket the best boost.

Fuel 1

1. Fill the base of the launch pad with baking soda. Add 1 tablespoon of vinegar to the rocket body. Quickly and carefully (so that the vinegar doesn't spill out!) turn the rocket over the opening of the base, so the parts fit snuggly together.
2. When you see bubbles foaming in the tube, it means your rocket is just about to launch. Step away from the rocket and see how high it goes!
3. If after two minutes, your rocket hasn't fired, then hold your rocket by the base, with the nose cone pointing outward and away from you. Pull the rocket from the base, rinse the two parts in warm water, and refuel your rocket.

Fuel 2

1. Use a rock to crush an Alka-Seltzer™ tablet into a fine powder. Pour the powder into the base of the launch pad.
2. Pour $1\frac{1}{2}$ tablespoon of warm water into the rocket body. Combine the water and Alka-Seltzer™, and launch as you did with Fuel 1.

Let's Speed it Up!

Now that you've launched your rocket, you can try some experiments that will make it blast off more quickly. Several factors can increase the rate of chemical reaction inside the rocket chamber. One thing that affects the rate of the reaction is the amount of surface of the solid that is in contact with the liquid fuel. Increasing the surface area of the solid increases the rate of the reaction. Another factor that affects the rate of the reaction is the temperature. You may find that the rocket will shoot off faster on warm days than on cold ones. Warming up the liquid fuel (vinegar or water) by placing it into a container inside a bowl of hot tap water will also cause the reaction to happen faster.

Try This:
Place a whole Alka-Seltzer™ tablet into a glass. Half fill the glass with water. Use a watch with a second hand to see how long it takes for the tablet to dissolve completely. Try this again using a crushed tablet instead of a solid one. Which one dissolves faster? Why?

How High Did it Go?

What goes up must come down, and your rocket is no exception. You can see it go up into the air, but how can you tell how high it goes? And can you make it go any higher? When the rocket goes up, there are two opposing, or opposite, forces acting on it. The first force is the push given by the escaping gas you produced when you mixed together the solid and liquid fuel. This force is pushing the rocket upward, away from the launching pad. The second force is gravity. Gravity is the force that the earth exerts as it pulls the rocket back to the ground. To make the rocket travel farther you need to increase the first force so it is stronger than the second force (you can't alter the force of gravity unless you travel to a different planet).

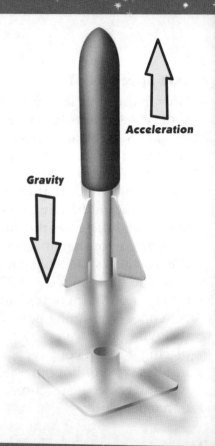

Acceleration

Gravity

Try This:

Cut a drinking straw with a pair of scissors to make a 3-inch piece. Thread a 40-foot piece of sewing thread or dental floss through the straw. Attach one end of the thread (with a piece of masking tape) to the rocket's launching pad. Tie the other end of the thread to a nearby pole or tree. Tape the straw to the side of your rocket with masking tape (avoid putting tape on the fins). Launch your rocket following the instructions on page 10. How far does the rocket go along the string? Try launching your rocket a couple of times using the hints on page 11. Does speeding up the launch make your rocket go farther?

Rockets Today

Rockets today have two main uses: for exploration of space and as vehicles for delivery of satellites. Space probes have been launched to investigate all the planets in our solar system except Pluto, and pictures have been sent back by the probes. The greatest distance was flown by the Voyager II space probe, which flew past Neptune, a distance of 2.8 billion miles! Scientists hope to soon see exciting new images of Mars and Saturn, as the probes to these planets report home. You may be able to see these pictures when they are displayed on the Internet, in magazines, or on television.

More and more, countries and even businesses are launching telecommunications and monitoring satellites into space. Improvements in rocket design have resulted in more powerful and versatile rockets being made for this purpose. It seems that even the sky *is not* the limit!

The Future of Rockets

Look how far rocket science has come in such a short time. It's been less than forty years since the first astronaut went into orbit around our planet, and rocket science has taken *giant* leaps forward. Scientists can now launch long-range missions into the farthest reaches of our solar system.

Where will rockets take us in the future? Rockets will take us to the far ends of the galaxy to explore space. People may build colonies on "new" planets and set up exciting scientific missions. Who knows? We may even discover intelligent life-forms in strange, new places. The more we explore space, the more we will learn about life on Earth and how the universe was created.

Try This:
Sometimes people think they have seen a UFO (unidentified flying object), when, in fact, it is a satellite flying overhead. Call a local observatory and ask them to tell you if any visible satellites will be passing over your home. If it is a clear night, you can see lights that are actually the satellites flying through space.

Where to Learn More

This kit is a simple and safe way to start learning about rockets. If you want to learn more about rockets, everything you need is on the Internet.

Check out NASA for the best in space. Try clicking on any links to "Education" or "Cool Links". You can even talk to an astronaut!
http://www.nasa.gov

When you are older, you may also wish to experiment with water rockets. These rockets are easy to build, but require close adult supervision! You can find information about water rockets on the Internet. Here's a place to start:
http://www.geocities.com/CapeCanaveral/Lab/5403

There are also model rocket clubs you can join, but you'll probably have to be old enough to drive a car before you join one of these clubs.
If you want to read about model rocketry, try this:
http://home.earthlink.net/~voraze/toc.html

Just remember, always practice safety when you are experimenting with rockets—and *ALWAYS* have fun!